Eradicating Singleton Anti-Patterns

Ensuring Efficient and Scalable Code

Table of Contents

Chapter 1. Introduction

In this Special Report titled "Eradicating Singleton Anti-Patterns: Ensuring Efficient and Scalable Code", we delve beneath the surface of some of the most deep-set coding practices. The Singleton pattern, handy yet controversial, has been widely adopted in programming without a true understanding of its impact on scalability and implications for your projects. However, our report doesn't dwell on the negative- it navigates these programming waters with practical elegance, offering solutions and guidance towards coding practices that are conducive to robust scalability. We've diligently broken down complex strategies into comprehensible dialogues, paving the way for both beginners and seasoned professionals alike. Get your hands on this Special Report, for it promises to elevate your understanding, foster more efficient coding practices, and propel you towards the path of truly scalable programming.

Chapter 2. Understanding Singleton Anti-Patterns

In the world of object-oriented programming (OOP), design patterns provide reusable solutions to recurrent problems. One such pattern, which sees widespread use, is the Singleton pattern. Despite its popularity and ease of use, it's often criticized for its implications on scalability and efficiency. To better understand this, it's crucial to first grasp the Singleton pattern and its typical implementation.

2.1. The Singleton Pattern

The Singleton pattern falls under the creational design patterns category and ensures that a class has only one instance, providing a global point of access to it. Here's a typical implementation of Singleton in Java:

```java
public class Singleton {
    private static Singleton uniqueInstance;
    private Singleton() {}
    public static synchronized Singleton getInstance() {
        if (uniqueInstance == null) {
            uniqueInstance = new Singleton();
        }
        return uniqueInstance;
    }
}
```

In the code snippet above, the Singleton class uses a private constructor to control instantiating the Singleton class. To get access to the Singleton object, it uses the 'getInstance()' method. If the Singleton instance does not exist, it is created. It then returns the

Singleton instance. The getInstance() method is synchronized to prevent two threads from accessing it simultaneously, which can lead to creating two Singleton instances.

2.2. Anti-Patterns and the Singleton

Programming methodologies, like design patterns, that are commonly utilized often have a reverse side: anti-patterns. An anti-pattern is a commonly reinvented but counterproductive design solution. They describe these solutions to typical problems which seem helpful initially, but can harm the project in the long term.

The Singleton pattern, although effective in controlling object creation and access, may possess some characteristics of an anti-pattern. The issues associated arise from the global state it introduces, potential multi-threading problems, hidden dependencies, and the difficulty in unit testing due to its nature.

2.3. The Global State Dilemma

A Singleton class inherently introduces a global state to the application, as the Singleton object's data remains in memory throughout the application run. Such global variables can risk data inconsistency since any part of the code can modify them. Most of the Singleton's problems revolve around the fact that it deviates from the tenets of two important principles of software engineering: the Single Responsibility Principle (SRP) and the Dependency Inversion Principle (DIP).

2.4. Tangles in Multi-threading

In multi-threaded applications, ensuring a single instance of a Singleton class can become challenging. Lazy initialization, as shown in the previous Java code snippet, can lead to race conditions if not synchronized correctly, resulting in multiple instances.

2.5. Hidden Dependencies

Singletons can disguise themselves as global variables and introduce hidden dependencies into your code. When instances are explicitly passed along, it's easy to spot the dependencies. However, with Singleton, you may not realize dependencies until the runtime crashes due to a missing Singleton.

2.6. Hurdles in Testing

Singleton's global nature makes it troublesome to use with unit tests. Singleton classes can maintain state between test cases and introduce unwanted dependencies, thereby making it difficult to set up and tear down test cases, which ideally should be independent.

2.7. Busting Singleton's Anti-Pattern Behavior

The Singleton isn't inherently evil, but using it incorrectly or extensively can lead to the issues discussed above. Here are some of the methods to avoid the Singleton anti-pattern:

2.8. Dependency Injection

Dependency Injection (DI) is a powerful alternative to Singleton. It allows objects to be dependent on abstract interfaces rather than concrete classes, making code more modular, flexible, and testing more straightforward.

For instance, in Java, the Spring framework's DI features provide mechanisms where instances can have singleton behavior but remain fully managed by the Spring context, allowing ease of testing and avoiding manual synchronization issues.

2.9. Using the Multiton Pattern

The Multiton pattern, an extension of the Singleton, allows operations on multiple instances based on keys. It maintains a List or Map of instances instead of a single variable.

For example in Java:

```java
public class Multiton {
    private static Map<String, Multiton> instances = new HashMap<>();
    private String name;
    private Multiton(String name) {this.name = name;}
    public static synchronized Multiton getInstance(String name) {
        if (!instances.containsKey(name)) {
            instances.put(name, new Multiton(name));
        }
        return instances.get(name);
    }
}
```

As with chosen solutions come considerations. You should be cautious using Multiton as creating too many instances can be a memory-intense operation.

2.10. Adopting the Scoped Singleton

A Scoped Singleton limits the instance to a certain scope, such as a thread or a session. This approach can help mitigate global state issues.

Analysing the costs and benefits of these alternatives will vary depending on your project's requirements. While Singleton might be a good fit for some applications, weighted use remains the keyword. Becoming aware of its nature as a potential anti-pattern and the options available to ensure the scalability and manageability of your code lets you make the best architectural decisions for your projects.

Chapter 3. The Origins and Popular Use of Singleton

The Singleton design pattern often has its roots traced back to the "Gang of Four," a moniker representing the four authors of the book "Design Patterns: Elements of Reusable Object-Oriented Software". Here, Singleton is categorized under the creational design pattern and is often touted as a straightforward solution when an application needs to have just one instance of a class.

However, its widespread adoption isn't entirely attributed to its recognitions in this book. The Singleton's popularity stems from its perceived simplicity. A system, an application, only requiring a singular instance of a class, seems intuitively easier to manage, and developers quickly turned to the Singleton when faced with such scenarios.

3.1. The Basics of Singleton Pattern

Singleton design pattern aims to ensure that a class has one, and only one, instance, and further provides a global point of access to this instance. The idea behind this pattern is pretty straightforward; it's about controlling object creation mechanisms. It is achieved by creating a class that can only be instantiated once, with that single instance accessible universally throughout the application.

At a high level, the basic structure of the Singleton pattern can be implemented in three steps:

1. Declare the default constructor to be private; this prevents other objects from using the 'new' operator with the Singleton class.

2. Create a static creation method that acts as a constructor. The 'static' keyword ensures that the method belongs to the class itself. This method would instantiate the Singleton class in an

exclusive way that only creates a new instance when one does not already exist.

3. Provide for a global point of access in terms of a public static method to get the Singleton instance.

This translated into code can be rendered successfully in virtually any object-oriented programming language.

3.2. One Instance, Many Problems

Despite the Singleton pattern seeming to be a panacea for dealing with single-instance classes, it quickly becomes a bottleneck when applications begin to scale. The argument against Singletons is multipronged. Most objections start with global state and issues related to it. Global state means that the instance could be accessed and potentially altered from anywhere in the application. The ability to change the global state facilitates tight coupling and can lead to inadvertent and hard-to-locate bugs.

Secondly, using Singleton invariably breaks the Single Responsibility Principle, a SOLID principle in object-oriented programming and design. The Singleton class, knowingly or not, takes on more than one responsibility. In addition to fulfilling its primary function, a Singleton is also responsible for managing its unique instance.

3.3. Overuse and Misunderstanding

Many times Singleton is used even when its specific use case is not required because it is perceived to be easier or the 'normal' way to do things. This is an issue since developers may no longer think about the effect of using Singleton. The line between when a Singleton is needed and when it's not needed blurs, consequently leading to its overuse.

Another challenge is the tendency to view Singleton as a global variable. Yes, it controls the instantiation to a single object, much like a global variable. But the Singleton pattern is more than just a global variable. Treating Singletons merely as global variables oversimplifies the design pattern, weakening the overall architecture.

Buddy Healthcare and Epic Games are great examples of companies that are known to use Singleton. These renowned companies may indicate that Singleton can indeed be a useful tool in some contexts, but contextual understanding is vital. These companies have teams of experienced developers who understand the implications, the cost, and the benefits of using something like a Singleton. Blindly adopting methods simply because successful companies are using them is a dangerous and misleading initiative.

3.4. Replacement for Singleton

With all the challenges with Singletons, the concept of Dependency Injection has gained traction as an alternative to Singleton. Dependency Injection (DI) is a design pattern that demonstrates how to create loosely coupled classes. It's not a direct alternative to Singleton, but it often arrives whenever there are discussions about Singleton's alternatives due to the aim to achieve similar purposes in a different, arguably more efficient manner.

DI brings high modularity, flexibility, and testability, addressing many Singleton pattern shortcomings. DI doesn't restrict your classes to be instanced only once but instead gives the programmer the power to control the number of instances. DI doesn't create dependencies between classes or results in tight coupling, which promotes ease of testing.

While this journey through the origins and popular use of Singleton has touched on many areas, it is not exhaustive. The objective was to present a comprehensive understanding that encourages developers to think beyond the Singleton pattern and consider other beneficial alternatives like Dependency Injection. Being able to discern the benefits, drawbacks, and implications of adopting any design pattern is a critical skill in software development. To understand Singletons in its entirety is to know when to use it, when not to use it, and, just as importantly, what to use in its place when necessary. The real challenge and art of programming lie not in mastering a design pattern but in understanding when and where it should be applied.

Chapter 4. Consequences of Singleton Misuse

No sooner than you have designed the Singleton pattern that you've set the wheels in motion for potential consequences, some of which may not be readily apparent. To fully appreciate the effects of Singleton misuse, it's necessary that we pull back the curtain and explore its intricacies, pitfalls, and unanticipated issues that are apt to crop up in programming projects.

4.1. The Illusion of Global Accessibility

Singletons provide a convenient means to access objects globally, and this becomes their raison d'être in many design situations. The idea of conveniently accessing methods and properties anywhere in the code seems handy indeed. However, this global accessibility can turn into an achilles' heel, leading to several issues:

1. Decreased modularity: Global objects, like Singletons, can be accessed and modified from any part of the code. However, this creates dependency and reduces the modularity of your code base. The stronger the dependency between code modules, the harder it becomes to modify, reuse or test them independently.

2. Unexpected behavior: Since any part of the code can modify a Singleton, it opens the door for inadvertent and unexpected behavior. Different parts of the code might attempt to utilize the Singleton differently, potentially causing conflicts.

3. Difficulties in multi-threaded situations: In the multithreaded environment, having globally accessible objects like Singletons can lead to issues related to synchronization and consistency, and hence, undesired results.

4.2. Failures in Testing and Mocking Singletons

Unit testing is a fundamental aspect of writing maintainable code, and Singletons introduce a number of obstacles in this area. The global nature of Singletons means that they keep their state for the lifetime of the application. So, one test can easily affect the outcome of another, leading to flaky tests that pass and fail intermittently, causing problems in Test-Driven Development (TDD) environments.

Further, Singletons make it hard to replace dependencies with mock objects. Substituting actual classes with mock objects is a common practice in unit testing. However, due to their global state, Singletons throw a wrench in the works when it comes to mocking dependencies. Overcoming this requires intricate work of setting appropriate state before and cleaning state after each test, leading to overheads and making the code clumsier to work with.

4.3. Compromised Scalability & Performance

In the context of a multi-threaded environment, Singleton misuse can lead to considerable performance bottlenecks. One of the most common issues surfaces when the Singleton object needs to be synchronized across multiple threads. The requirement of locking a Singleton object to maintain thread safety can lead to concurrency issues and a significant decrease in performance, mainly when it is frequently accessed from multiple threads.

Moreover, the global nature of Singletons tends to promote a stateful programming style. Stateful components make it difficult to scale horizontally because they necessitate data synchronization among various nodes in a clustered environment, impacting the overall performance and scalability.

4.4. Violation of Single Responsibility Principle (SRP)

The Single Responsibility Principle (SRP) is a SOLID principle of OOP design. It posits that a class should have one reason to change. Singleton classes often find themselves loaded with multiple responsibilities - acting as a global point of access and simultaneously handling its business responsibilities.

This dual-task often leads Singletons into becoming a God Object: an object that knows too much or does too much. The state and behavior of God Objects are usually complex and can cause a nightmare for maintenance.

4.5. Difficulty in Subclassing

Singletons can often pose challenges to inheritance or subclassing. The primary reason comes from their very nature- a Singleton allowing a single instance for a class. It makes it hard to create a subclass because it involves complex process to ensure its associated base class Singleton object also respects the same restriction.

A Singleton base class has to be modified each time a subclass needs to be Singleton. This can create unnecessary complexity and implies that Singletons tend to be a closed design. In such a scenario, it violates the Open/Closed principle, a part of SOLID design principles, which states that Objects should be open for extension but closed for modification.

To remediate the effects of Singleton misuse, we can harness different approaches such as using Dependency Injection (DI), utilizing Service Locator pattern, having scoped Singletons, creating stateless Singletons, and applying other design practices.

However, it's essential to understand that replacement solutions for

Singletons should consider the specific characteristics and requirements of the project. Without careful consideration, we might end up bringing in new complexities. Thus, understanding alternatives to Singletons is just as crucial as understanding the Singleton pattern itself.

Singletons, when used judiciously, can prove beneficial. The key lies in understanding when it is appropriate to use this pattern and assessing the potential long-term implications on your code base's maintainability, testability, and scalability.

Chapter 5. Analyzing the Impact on Scalability and Efficiency

To delve deeper into the implications of the Singleton pattern, let's first look at what constraints and issues arise when it's implemented, particularly focusing on scalability and efficiency.

5.1. The Nature of Singleton and Impact on Scalability

The Singleton pattern is designed to ensure that a class has only a single instance, with a global point of access to it. While in some scenarios, having one instance is genuinely beneficial, these situations are more uncommon than you might think. The idea of limiting an object to a single instance can impede scalability, primarily in a multi-threaded environment because when multiple threads need access to the singleton instance, they may need to wait until they acquire a lock on the object, potentially hampering performance.

Additionally, singletons often become a global point for various disparate parts of a program to interface with, which may lead to complicated dependencies and difficulty in changing parts of the program independently later on. This rigidity might have consequences in terms of scalability, as inflexible architecture may struggle to scale up efficiently when your project grows.

5.2. Impact of Singleton on Testability and Efficiency

In terms of testability and hence the efficiency of your development process, singletons can pose some significant challenges. In most cases, unit testing requires that the units of software under test have no dependencies, or that the dependencies can be simulated. However, due to the global nature of the singleton, this pattern can introduce implicit dependencies in your code that are hard to isolate, potentially leading to difficulties in setting up and executing unit tests.

Moreover, since Singleton objects often carry state from one part of your code to another, defining precise testing environments can become tricky. Mocking singletons proves even more problematic, as these objects are not initially designed to be instantiated more than once. Thus, the Singleton pattern can decrease the efficiency of the development process.

5.3. Judicious Use and Alternatives

Despite its drawbacks, the Singleton pattern is not entirely deprecated. There can be cases and scenarios where its adoption is a lesser evil. For example, when dealing with limited resources or hardware access, using the Singleton pattern can be an appropriate solution. However, you should be very judicious about such use, always considering the impacts on scalability and maintainability of the code.

Instead of singletons, one can often use Dependency Injection (DI) to supply all parts of an application with the shared resources they need. DI foregrounds the dependencies an object has, making them explicit and defined in one place.

Another alternative is the 'bunch of stateless methods' (also known as utility class) pattern. This pattern invokes a class, where all data lives in automatic variables, and no class-level data persists between individual function calls. It helps eliminate the testing issues associated with Singleton and provide better scalability.

5.4. Pragmatic Approach to Code Design

While various design patterns, including Singletons and their alternatives, provide firm starting points, it's crucial to approach your code design pragmatically and sensibly. Rather than strictly adhering to one pattern or avoiding another, it is always better to perceive these patterns as tools in your toolkit, using the appropriate tool for the job at hand.

In conclusion, while Singletons bring a fair share of challenges and limitations to the table, particularly regarding scalability and testability, you can mitigate these challenges by using alternatives like DI or utility classes, or even Singletons themselves in a judicious manner, applied only where appropriate. It's critical always to consider the specific needs of your project, prioritize effective communication within your code, and remain flexible and open to using the right tool for the job.

Remember: design patterns are the means, not the end. Your goal is writing clear, maintainable, scalable code that solves the problem you are addressing. As a developer, your challenge and opportunity is to balance the use of these patterns in service of that central goal.

Chapter 6. Reconstructing Perspectives: When to and When Not to Use Singletons

Understanding the Singleton pattern's place in your coding toolkit requires an in-depth exploration of its use-cases, benefits, and pitfalls. We'll start by digging into scenarios where implementing the Singleton pattern is advantageous, followed by instances where it may obstruct scalability and efficient development.

6.1. Deciphering Singleton's Significance

The Singleton pattern finds purpose in scenarios where you require exactly one instance of a class. A key strength of this pattern is its provision of global access, reducing the need for passing references to the object throughout your application. Delegation of responsibilities to Singleton is efficient as you ensure one central controlling factor, which can be beneficial in maintaining operations like logging, driver objects, caching, thread pools, and database connections.

Yet, it is the very global state of Singletons that is its Achille's heel. As we navigate through the sea of code, global state is often an enemy hiding beneath the surface.

6.2. Appreciating the Perks

To understand when to employ Singleton, we have to understand its strengths:

- **Controlled access to a sole instance**: Singleton restricts initializing the object to one instance, providing a global point of access to it. This can be useful for coordinating actions across the system.

- **Flexible Interface**: Just because Singleton forces single instance doesn't mean it forbids storing more than one. This flexibility of accommodating more instances, if needed, can be beneficial.

6.3. Comprehending the Caveats

If overused or misused, Singleton can add unnecessary complexity to your codebase, adversely impact performance, and hampers testing. Some of the critical issues inherent to Singletons include:

- **Global Variables**: Singletons could easily be misused as substitutes for global variables, opening the door to problematic global states.

- **Concurrency Issues**: Singleton does not inherently cater to multi-threaded environments, inviting potential problems in code's scalability.

- **Difficulty in Testing**: Since Singletons maintain state during the lifecycle of an application, they make unit tests tough to write and understand.

6.4. Shedding Light on Suitable Scenarios

Now that we have established the strengths and weaknesses, let's examine the situations that call for the use of Singletons.

- **Logger Classes**: Used to log messages for debugging or information tracking purposes, Logger classes usually employ Singleton because it's not resource intensive and offers a unified access point.

- **Configuration Classes**: Configuration settings used throughout your application signify another apt application of the Singleton pattern. It can avoid redundant operations like reading the configuration data from a file for every request.

6.5. Identifying Inappropriate Instances

Conversely, there are situations when using a Singleton is far from optimal:

- **Database Connections**: While it might seem appealing to have a Singleton manage your database connection, it can lead to bottlenecks in a multi-threaded environment, hampering scalability.

- **Object-Oriented Classes**: Objects interacting with each other should refrain from using Singleton as it introduces tight coupling and hinders unit testing.

6.6. Concluding Thoughts

Singletons are a useful design pattern, but can easily be misused or overused. While they provide instance control and global access, they can lead to hidden dependencies, hinder testing, and create difficulties in maintaining multi-threaded environments.

The Singleton pattern's right application requires wisdom to understand where the balance lies - which comes with knowing your project's needs and the consequent impact on codebase's viability and scalability. Ensure to weigh the pros and cons while deciding its implementation.

The Singleton pattern is a classic representation of "Just because you can, doesn't mean you should." As we traverse the vast realm of coding, it becomes essential to veer clear of the mesmerizing aura of design patterns and identify them as tools, using them only where they are truly the best fit.

Despite its allure, Singleton must not become the default design pattern for every codebase - allowing the problem's unique context to dictate your choice of pattern is the key to efficient, adaptable, and scalable coding.

Chapter 7. Alternatives to Singleton: Exploring Patterns & Techniques

In application design, it's normal to encounter scenarios that require a single, shared instance of a class. Among global variables, databases, caches, thread pools, and registries, the notion of a singular object is far from foreign in programming. The Singleton pattern has proven to be a popular response to these needs, but it's not without its share of controversial baggage. Its misuse, misunderstanding, and subtle complexity can turn it from a practical solution to a liability. This chapter delves into other design patterns and techniques that serve as viable alternatives to Singleton.

7.1. Monostate/Borg Pattern

Starting with the Monostate (Borg in Python) pattern, which gives a pseudo-Singleton behavior. Here, instead of having only one instance like in Singleton, you create any number of instances you need but they all share the same state. This way, Singleton's complexities are resolved but the intention remains.

In Python, an example would look like this:

```python
class Borg:
    _shared_state = {}

    def __init__(self):
        self.__dict__ = self._shared_state
```

In this pattern, the `_shared_state` class variable is essentially what each instance reference when they check the internal dictionary. This means that while there may be various instances, they're all using the same `_shared_state`.

7.2. Dependency Injection

Next, we look at Dependency Injection (DI) - a powerful way to handle the single instance requirement. In DI, instead of having the components manage their dependencies, these dependencies are "injected" into them by an external entity (i.e., a container or a builder). Dependencies, in this case, could be anything that a component depends on for functioning, for instance, services, configurations, or other components.

This way, single instances (services/objects) are created and managed by a container that injects these instances into the components using them. This promotes decoupling, easier testing, and better maintainable code. Most modern frameworks like Spring (Java), .NET, or Angular provide out of the box DI containers.

7.3. The Factory Method Pattern

The Factory Method Pattern deviates from using Singleton by creating an object through a factory method, either specified in an interface and implemented by child classes or implemented in a base class and optionally overridden by derived classes. This gives you more flexibility in what gets instantiated, providing a sophisticated way to decouple your client code from the concrete classes.

Here is an example in Java:

```java
public abstract class AnimalFactory {
    protected abstract Animal createAnimal();

    public Animal getAnimal() {
        Animal animal = createAnimal();
```

```
        animal.feed();
    }
}
```

Here, `AnimalFactory` is your base factory class with the `createAnimal()` factory method. This method is called in `getAnimal()`, which also calls the `feed()` method on the animal. Subclasses would then override `createAnimal()` to create their animals.

7.4. Multiton Pattern

Close to Singleton, the Multiton Pattern broadens the concept of a singleton by allowing a predefined set number of instances, each represented by a key. In Java, a multiton could be represented by a `HashMap`, with the key being a string identifier for the instance, and the value being the instance itself.

Although less used, Multiton can also introduce new problems – especially regarding memory use. Hence, it should be used judiciously.

These explored alternatives not only provide the simplicity of a single instance (Singleton) but also tend to evade typical Singleton problems such as global state sharing, testability issues, and threading bugs. Understanding them enhances the capabilities of a programmer, aiding in making decisions that better align with the specific need of the program, ultimately delivering efficient and scalable code.

Chapter 8. Diving into Multiton and Dependency Injection

If you're already familiar with the Singleton pattern, you might know about its stricter cousin – the Multiton pattern. The Multiton pattern controls object creation by enabling a class to have only a limited palette of instances, whereas the Singleton allows just one. Along with this, the concept of Dependency Injection (DI), which is a technique whereby one object (or static method) supplies the dependencies of another object – comes into play. This is a key aspect of many current software designs, including object-oriented programming (OOP) and functional programming.

8.1. The Multiton Pattern at a Glance

In traditional Singleton structures, the class controls the instantiation process by keeping a private static variable to hold its singular instance, ensuring no other potential instances are created. The Multiton pattern extends this concept, utilizing a mapped structure to oversee the creation and accessibility of multiple instances.

Consider an application requiring different database connections. Implementing a Singleton could resolve the constructor overload. This way, the necessary details for each connection would be provided without hindering the number of connections. In this structure, the Singleton instance will encompass a map where keys correspond to unique instances of the class.

8.2. Dependency Injection: A Contemporary Solution

Dependency Injection, often simplified to DI, is a software design pattern that manages class dependencies. In DI, an object receives other objects that it depends on, referred to as dependencies. You aren't creating objects but describing how they should be created.

The technique relies on the concept of "Inversion of Control," which contends that custom-written portions of a computer program receive the flow of control from a generic framework. DI achieves this by removing the dependency from the actual code and providing it from an external source.

8.3. Multiton and Dependency Injection: The Link

Multiton and Dependency Injection can be perceived as two sides of the same coin in the realm of efficient and scalable code development.

Both routes direct programmers towards more scalable, efficient methods of object creation and management. With Multiton, it's about smart and streamlined object instance handling, delivering each instance as necessary without unnecessary new instances. As for Dependency Injection, it's about clean, flexible, and modular code that's conducive to reusability and maintainability, keeping the architecture loose and flexible, with high segregation of concerns.

8.4. Implementing the Multiton Pattern

Let's delve into how to implement the Multiton pattern. For illustration, let's consider a scenario where we have a print spooler that can handle different print queues.

```java
class PrintSpooler {

    private static final Map<String, PrintSpooler>
instances = new HashMap<>();

    private PrintSpooler() {
    }

    public static PrintSpooler getInstance(String key) {
        instances.computeIfAbsent(key, k -> new
PrintSpooler());
        return instances.get(key);
    }

    //other methods
}
```

In the scenario above, an instance of PrintSpooler is created based on a key using the computeIfAbsent method, which makes sure we don't create unnecessary additional instances.

This implementation resembles the Singleton pattern but instead manages multiple instances in a Map data structure to track the different print queues.

8.5. Implementing Dependency Injection (DI)

Dependency Injection can be implemented in multiple ways, primarily through constructors, methods, or fields. However, the constructor-based DI is the most commonly recommended.

Consider an instance where we have two classes named `ClientService` and `Service`.

```java
public class ClientService {
    private Service service;

    public ClientService(Service service) {
        this.service = service;
    }

    public void work() {
        // use service
    }
}

public class Service {
    // service implementation
}
```

In this example, a `ClientService` instance requires a `Service` instance to operate correctly – this is our dependency. Rather than having `ClientService` instantiate a new `Service` itself – which makes testing difficult and binds the two classes' lifecycles – the `ClientService` constructor requests an instance of `Service`. This way, `ClientService` can work with any `Service` instance, and the lifecycle of the `Service` class is independent of `ClientService`.

8.6. Multiton, Dependency Injection, and Pitfalls to Avoid

Despite the improvements in scalability and efficiency, there are pitfalls and potential roadblocks associated with both Multiton and DI that developers must keenly avoid.

1. Ensuring Instance Safety: With Multiton, you must ensure instance safety. If the getInstance method is called from multiple threads simultaneously, it may create multiple objects in a multi-threaded environment, contrary to our design. Implement synchronization safely and correctly.

2. Managing Instance Uniqueness: In Multiton, ensure that instance uniqueness is not broken by cloning or serialization.

3. Over-Engineering: With DI, avoid over-engineering. Not every single class or object requires injection. If an object is used only in one place or doesn't contain any important business logic, it need not be managed via DI.

4. Tight-Coupling: Mind that DI doesn't become a method to simply shift responsibilities and create other forms of tight coupling.

Using these tools judiciously can turn around development cycles, making them more efficient, scalable, and successful. With the right knowledge, developers can drive their codebases toward being more sustainable and maintanable, shaping the future of the programming world one line of code at a time.

Chapter 9. Refactoring Singleton Ridden Code

As codebases mature, they tend to accumulate vestiges of sub-optimal design decisions made during their inception or development. Interestedly, Singleton patterns often surface as these relics. Notwithstanding their perceived utility of ensuring that only one instance of a class exists, which aids in controlling access to shared resources, they often display anti-pattern behaviors. Let's delve into how to refactor Singleton ridden code, effectively elevating it from the shackles of constrained scalability.

9.1. Understanding the Problem Space

Singletons, while solving certain problems, can introduce profound issues. They make code hard to reason about due to hidden dependencies, enable global variables, and make parallel testing challenging, thus ruining testability. To refactor such code, you must pinpoint the Singletons lurking within and understand their impact on scalability and overall code health.

9.2. Identifying Singletons

Crucially, code inspections are required to identify potential Singletons up for refactoring. This manual scanning process considers characteristics typical to Singletons such as private constructors, static methods, and instance variables.

```
public class Singleton {
    private static Singleton uniqueInstance;
```

```
    private Singleton() {}

    public static synchronized Singleton getInstance() {
        if (uniqueInstance == null) {
            uniqueInstance = new Singleton();
        }
        return uniqueInstance;
    }
}
```

Always be attentive to more subtle Singleton presentations, which slightly deviate from the archetypal scenario.

9.3. Deciding on Evaluation Metrics

Maintaining independent system components ensures scalability and flexibility. Singleton-associated issues distort this independence, causing code rigidities. Thus, our evaluation metrics should pivot towards identifying and eliminating these rigidities to facilitate broader scalability.

9.4. Refactoring Strategy Outline

Refactoring Singleton-infested code goes beyond simply substitifying Singletons with non-Singleton classes. Rather, it revolves around altering the granular details of the codebase with methods such as dependency injection, abstract factories, and service locator patterns.

9.5. Adopting Dependancy Injection

Dependency Injection (DI) is one powerful strategy to replace Singletons. In DI, objects are passed dependencies during creation rather than acquiring them on their own, enhancing the code's testability and efficiency.

```java
public class SingletonClient {
    private final Singleton singleton;

    public SingletonClient(Singleton singleton) {
        this.singleton = singleton;
    }
}
```

While the simplicity of DI is palpable, its implementation may necessitate a considerable amount of code changes. For this, DI frameworks like Spring or Guice come to the rescue, offering easy mechanisms to handle such construction logic at a central location.

9.6. Leveraging Abstract Factories

Although DI offers a solution, its broad application might complicate testing and development. Here, Abstract Factories can be employed, encapsulating the creation of complex objects while ensuring single instances where needed.

```java
public class SingletonFactory {
    private Singleton singleton;

    public Singleton getSingletonInstance() {
        if (singleton == null) {
            singleton = new Singleton();
        }
        return singleton;
    }
}
```

The Abstract Factory facilitates instance control while eliminating the global access predicament. However, take care that factories do not become unwieldy, complicating the code.

9.7. Implementing Service Locator Pattern

Service Locator Pattern provides a registry to acquire dependencies, thus a suitable Singleton alternative whilst maintaining control over instantiation dynamics.

```java
public class ServiceLocator {
    private static ServiceLocator instance;
    private final Singleton singleton;

    private ServiceLocator() {
        singleton = new Singleton();
    }

    public static synchronized ServiceLocator
getInstance() {
        if(instance == null) {
            instance = new Singleton();
        }
        return instance;
    }

    public Singleton getSingletonService() {
        return singleton;
    }
}
```

It smoothly fits into the codebase, enabling the replacement of Singletons without significant codebase alteration. However, it's wise to keep a close eye for potential chaos in the absence of a standardized approach to service registration and lookup.

9.8. Keeping Scalability in Focus

Efficient refactoring is guided by the North Star of scalability, ensuring codebases remain flexible and efficient as they scale up. Regardless of the methods employed, keeping scalability in focus is paramount for this endeavor.

9.9. Conclusion

Singleton Patterns, while popular, can embed unsavory scalability limitations into your code. Recognizing these pitfalls and adopting strategies such as Depedency Injection, Abstract Factories, and Service Locator Pattern can help you significantly improve your codebases' scalability. By consistently centering your approach around scalability, you can ensure that your refactor effectively prepares your code for the demands of tomorrow.

Chapter 10. Best Practices for Scalable and Efficient Code

Scalable and efficient coding is an aspect of development that reaches far beyond the individual developer's code. It is about making sure that your solutions deploy effectively in a production environment, especially when dealing with high volumes of data or traffic. Let's start by exploring some of the general practices that every developer should incorporate into their daily routine.

10.1. Code Understandability

First of all, it's vital that code is easy to understand. It's not just you who needs to understand your code, it's also other developers who need to use or modify your code in the future.

Writing self-documenting code is one of the best approaches to improve code understandability. This involves:

- Clear naming conventions: Function and variable names should accurately describe their intentions or data they hold.

- Use of constants: If a value is repeated multiple times in your code, declare it as a constant.

- Keeping functions and classes small: Each function and class should have a single responsibility.

- Consistent formatting: Consistent indentation, spacing, and brackets improve the readability of code significantly.

10.2. Maintainability and Flexibility

Maintainable code is modular and loosely coupled. This means your code should be organized in such a way that changing one part of it doesn't automatically necessitate changes in other parts.

Flexibility means code can be easily extended or changed. To ensure this:

- Avoid hard coding: Don't use constants directly in computations or logic within functions.

- Use abstractions: Abstract out the functionality that could possibly change in the future.

To improve maintainability and flexibility, programmers should:

- Keep modules encapsulated

- Keep functions as pure as they can, which means minimize side effects.

- Use established design patterns where applicable.

10.3. Optimizing for Performance

Optimization refers to the process of modifying a system to make it work more efficiently or use fewer resources. In computer science, the term is typically used to describe the efforts to make the execution time of a computer program or the size of a data structure as small as possible.

Here are some ways to optimize for performance:

- Use efficient data structures: Make sure to use the most efficient data structure for your particular task, be it linked lists, arrays, hash maps, or trees.

- Algorithm selection: Consider the time and space complexities while choosing an algorithm.

- Optimize database queries: When dealing with databases, an un-optimized query can have a dramatic impact on performance.

Use correct indexes, avoid n+1 query problems, and take advantage of caching when possible.

10.4. Dealing with Errors

Expecting and handling errors properly is often overlooked, leading to many potential pitfalls. Here are some practices to properly deal with errors:

- Fail fast: If something goes wrong in your application, the software should ideally stop immediately, making the error as obvious as possible.

- Throw exceptions: When detected in unexpected situations, rather than handling them silently and causing potential future issues.

- Use descriptive error messages: It makes errors easier to understand and resolve.

10.5. Testing

Testing verifies that our code works as expected and makes sure the changes we introduce don't break the existing functionality. To adopt good testing practices:

- Write unit tests: They test a unit of code, often a function or a method, in isolation.

- Write integration tests: They test the interaction between different parts of your code.

- Automate your tests: Automated tests can be run regularly, preferably before each commit to the code repository.

10.6. Code Reviews

Code reviews can iron out many problems even before the code goes into the testing phase. Some tips for effective code reviews:

- Review code for understandability, maintainability, scalability, and testability.

- It should be performed by the developer's peers.

- Encourage developers to explain their solution as a part of the code review process.

Each of these practices significantly enhances code scalability and efficiency. As developers, we must understand that code isn't written once; it's read, updated, optimized and maintained over time. By adhering to these practices, it ensures this process is as smooth as possible and programmes are truly scalable. There are, of course, many other practices to ponder upon and much more to learn, but applying the concepts discussed above will certainly put you ahead in the journey towards efficient coding.

Chapter 11. Case Studies: Triumphs and Downfalls of Singleton Usage

Singleton, a design pattern that restricts object creation to a sole instance, can be either an effective tool or a recipe for disaster if misunderstood. In this chapter, we will engage in a discourse by studying real-world scenarios where this particular pattern played prominent parts. This thorough examination will provide insights into when to use Singleton, how to use it appropriately, and the repercussions when its usage is mismanaged.

11.1. The Triumph of Logging Systems

A widespread yet extraordinary application of the Singleton pattern is in Logging systems. It is absolutely imperative that the application writing logs uses the same instance throughout its lifespan to avoid inconsistencies and to maintain chronological order.

Consider a multithreaded financial system application that handles multiple banking transactions. A flaw in the logging system can make it difficult to troubleshoot when concurrent transactions cause an unexpected exception. Using the Singleton pattern ensures that all logs are written using the same instance, ensuring their chronological order in the log file.

The simplistic elegance of Singleton in preserving the order of logs is a great example of where the pattern shines. It prevents concurrent processes from creating disjointed logs, thereby ensuring a consistent data flow that is crucial for performance monitoring and debugging.

```java
public class Logger {
    private static Logger instance;

    private Logger(){}

    public static synchronized Logger getInstance() {
        if (instance == null) {
            instance = new Logger();
        }
        return instance;
    }

    public void log(String message) {
        // Log message method
    }
}
```

11.2. The Downfall in Multithreaded Environments

The Singleton pattern's strengths become its potential drawbacks in certain contexts. One such context is a multithreaded environment. The very principle that makes Singleton powerful- having only one instance- can make it a liability in these situations.

Let's contemplate a scenario where an ecommerce web application uses Singleton for database connectivity. Considering that thousands of users make simultaneous requests, the shared Singleton instance for connecting to the database becomes a significant bottleneck.

```java
public class DatabaseConn {
    private static DatabaseConn instance;
    private Connection conn;
```

```java
    private DatabaseConn() throws SQLException {
        String url, username, password; // Set database
details
        this.conn = DriverManager.getConnection(url,
username, password);
    }

    public static synchronized DatabaseConn
getInstance() throws SQLException{
        if (instance == null) {
            instance = new DatabaseConn();
        }
        return instance;
    }
}
```

The getInstance() method ensures there is only one instance. However, due to high concurrency, this instance ends up being shared across numerous threads, leading to performance degradation and potential data conflicts.

11.3. Triumphs in Configuration Settings

Singleton shines in scenarios where the system needs to fetch configurations from a single source. A common instance is reading configuration files during runtime.

A web application that needs to fetch various API keys, URLs, or system-wide settings at runtime stands to benefit significantly from the Singleton pattern. Encapsulating the configuration settings within a Singleton object ensures consistency throughout the application's runtime, and reduces I/O latency by persisting the data in memory after the initial load.

```java
public class Configuration {
    private static Configuration instance;
    private Properties properties;

    private Configuration(){
        properties = new Properties();
        try {
            properties.load(new
FileInputStream("config.properties"));
        } catch (IOException e) {
            e.printStackTrace();
        }
    }

    public static synchronized Configuration
getInstance() {
        if (instance == null) {
            instance = new Configuration();
        }
        return instance;
    }

    public String getProperty(String key) {
        return properties.getProperty(key);
    }
}
```

11.4. Downfalls in Testing and Maintainability

While Singleton has its remarkable uses, it also poses profound challenges in software testing and maintainability. Since a Singleton's lifecycle is concurrent with the application, it tends to persist data from one test case to another, leading to inconsistencies and hard-to-debug errors.

In addition, overuse of Singleton can make code harder to understand and maintain. The global access provided by Singleton means that any part of the software can change its state. When dealing with large codebases, this level of freedom can hamper source code comprehensibility, leaving a trail of code that is hard to follow and tweak.

Conclusively, the Singleton design pattern is a forceful tool when implemented judiciously. Recognizing its strengths and potential pitfalls can guide a programmer towards writing scalable and maintainable code. The case studies detailed out should help you make an informed decision when considering adopting Singleton in your projects. It's all about understanding the requirements, constraints, and with that knowledge, maneuvering the Singleton design pattern in the right direction.

9 798856 061658